Numbers with Bella

Lorraine O'Garro

Published by Melanin Origins LLC
PO Box 122123; Arlington, TX 76012

First Edition

Library of Congress Control Number: 2017911669

ISBN: 9781626768635 hardback
ISBN: 9781626768666 paperback
ISBN: 9781626768673 ebook

Dedicated to Myla and Mia

Sun

Palm Trees

African Drums

Candles

Coconuts

Starfish

Pyramids

Spider Legs

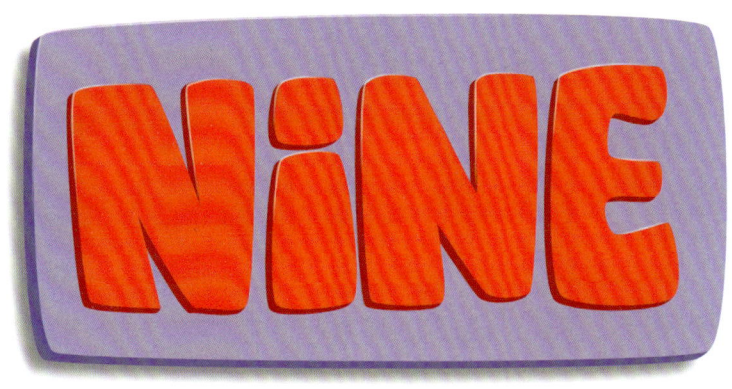

Balloons

Toes

To learn more with Bella visit learnwithbella.com